Disclaimer:

I0454515

The information provided in this book, "Cybersecurity Simplified, A beginners guide to Protecting your Digital World," is intended for general informational purposes only. While every effort has been made to ensure the accuracy and clarity of the content, the author and publisher make no representations or warranties of any kind, express or implied, about the completeness, accuracy, reliability, suitability, or availability concerning the information, products, services, or related graphics contained in this book for any purpose.

The content of this book is not a substitute for professional cybersecurity advice or guidance. Readers are encouraged to consult with cybersecurity experts, professionals, or other qualified authorities for advice specific to their individual situations. The author and publisher disclaim any liability for any loss or damage, including without limitation, indirect or consequential loss or damage, or any loss or damage whatsoever arising from loss of data or profits arising out of, or in connection with, the use of this book.

The inclusion of external links or references to third-party websites, products, or services does not imply endorsement or recommendation. The author and publisher are not responsible for the content, privacy practices, or actions of third-party websites or services.

Readers are encouraged to exercise their own judgment and discretion when applying the information provided in this book. The author and publisher shall not be held responsible for any negative consequences resulting from the use of the information presented herein.

By reading this book, readers acknowledge and agree to the terms of this disclaimer.

CYBERSECURITY SIMPLIFIED

A Beginner's Guide to protecting your Digital World

Welcome to "Cybersecurity Simplified," a comprehensive guide crafted for beginners eager to navigate the digital landscape securely. In this book, we will demystify the fundamentals of cybersecurity, providing easy-to-understand concepts and practical instructions to help you fortify your digital presence.

CHAPTER 1: UNDERSTANDING CYBERSECURITY

In this chapter, we'll introduce you to the basics of cybersecurity, what it is, why it matters, and how it impacts your daily life. We'll break down common terms and set the foundation for a secure online journey.

CHAPTER 2: CREATING STRONG PASSWORDS

Learn the art of crafting robust passwords and securing your online accounts. This chapter includes simple tips for password creation, management, and the importance of unique passwords for each account.

CHAPTER 3: RECOGNIZING PHISHING ATTACKS

Discover the sneaky world of phishing and how to spot deceptive attempts to steal your information. We'll provide practical guidance on identifying phishing emails and protecting yourself from online scams.

CHAPTER 4: SECURING YOUR DEVICES
Explore easy-to-follow steps for securing your computer, smartphone, and tablet. Learn about updates, antivirus software, and basic security settings to keep your devices safe from potential threats.

CHAPTER 5: SOCIAL MEDIA SAFETY
Navigate the social media landscape with confidence. This chapter covers privacy settings, recognizing social engineering tactics, and securing your social media accounts to enjoy a positive online experience.

CHAPTER 6: DATA BACKUPS AND RECOVERY
Discover the importance of data backups and how to safeguard your digital treasures. We'll guide you through different backup methods and recovery planning to ensure your data remains intact.

CHAPTER 7: STAYING SAFE ON PUBLIC WI-FI
Learn the risks associated with public Wi-Fi and how to protect yourself when connecting to these networks. We'll introduce the concept of VPNs and share practical tips for safe online browsing.

CHAPTER 8: RECOGNIZING ONLINE SCAMS
Uncover common online scams and arm yourself with knowledge to avoid falling victim. This chapter provides red flags, protective measures, and reporting tools to stay one step ahead of cybercriminals.

CHAPTER 9: SAFEGUARDING YOUR PERSONAL IDENTITY
Understand the significance of your personal identity and explore practical steps to protect it online. This chapter covers securing documents, monitoring credit reports, and recognizing phishing attempts.

CHAPTER 10: CREATING A SECURE ONLINE PRESENCE

Wrap up your cybersecurity journey by learning how to build a positive and secure online presence. From choosing strong usernames to engaging in positive online communities, this chapter empowers you to navigate the digital world responsibly.

Chapter 1: Understanding Cybersecurity

Welcome to the exciting world of cybersecurity! In this chapter, we'll embark on a journey to unravel the mysteries of digital security and lay the groundwork for a safer online experience. Whether you're new to the digital realm or seeking to enhance your cybersecurity knowledge, this chapter will provide you with a solid foundation.

What is Cybersecurity?

At its core, cybersecurity is the practice of protecting computers, networks, and data from digital threats. These threats can come in various forms, from malicious software and hackers to phishing attempts and other cybercrimes. The goal of cybersecurity is to ensure the confidentiality, integrity, and availability of information in the digital space.

Key Concepts:

1. Confidentiality:

Protecting information from unauthorized access ensures that your sensitive data remains private and secure.

2. Integrity:

Maintaining the accuracy and trustworthiness of data is crucial. Cybersecurity aims to prevent unauthorized alterations to information.

3. Availability:

Cybersecurity measures also focus on ensuring that data and systems are available when needed, preventing disruptions and downtime.

Why Cybersecurity Matters

In our increasingly interconnected world, cybersecurity plays a vital role in safeguarding personal, financial, and sensitive information. Without proper security measures, individuals and organizations are vulnerable to a range of cyber threats, including identity theft, financial fraud, and data breaches.

The Digital Landscape:
1. Personal Devices:
Your computer, smartphone, tablet, and other devices store a wealth of personal information. Cybersecurity helps protect this data from unauthorized access.

2. Online Transactions:
Whether you're shopping online, banking, or accessing medical records, cybersecurity ensures the security of your transactions and sensitive information.

3. Social Media:
Social media platforms, while great for connecting with others, pose cybersecurity risks. Understanding these risks is essential for a safe and enjoyable online presence.

Cybersecurity is for Everyone:
Cybersecurity is not reserved for experts or tech enthusiasts—it's for everyone. This book is designed with beginners in mind, providing easy-to-understand explanations and practical tips to empower you to take control of your digital security.

What You'll Learn:
1. Common Cyber Threats:
Explore the landscape of digital threats, including viruses, malware, phishing attacks, and more.

2. Basic Security Measures:
Learn fundamental cybersecurity practices to protect your devices and personal information.

3. Safe Online Behaviour:
Understand the do's and don'ts of online behaviour to minimize the risk of falling victim to cybercrimes.

As we dive into the realm of cybersecurity, remember that knowledge is your greatest ally. By understanding the principles of cybersecurity and adopting best practices, you're taking the first steps towards a safer and more secure digital journey. In the chapters to come, we'll explore specific aspects of cybersecurity, providing you with the tools and insights needed to navigate the digital landscape with confidence.

Chapter 2: Creating Strong Passwords

In the digital age, passwords are your first line of defence against unauthorized access to your accounts and personal information. In this chapter, we'll delve into the art of creating strong and secure passwords, helping you build robust barriers against potential cyber threats.

Your passwords act as virtual keys, granting access to your online accounts. Weak or easily guessable passwords can leave you vulnerable to unauthorized access, identity theft, and other cybercrimes. By understanding how to create strong passwords, you enhance your overall cybersecurity posture.

Characteristics of Strong Passwords:
1. Length:
Aim for passwords with a minimum of 12 characters. Longer passwords are generally more secure.

2. Complexity:
Include a mix of uppercase and lowercase letters, numbers, and special characters to increase complexity.

3. Unpredictability:
Avoid using easily guessable information such as birthdays, names, or common words. Opt for combinations that are not easily associated with you.

Creating a Strong Password
1. Passphrases:
Consider using passphrases—longer combinations of words or a sentence. For example, "MountainSunset@2023" is both strong and memorable.

2. Avoid Common Passwords:
Steer clear of commonly used passwords like "password," "123456," or "qwerty." These are easy targets for attackers.

3. Unique for Each Account:
 Avoid using the same password across multiple accounts. If one account is compromised, having unique passwords limits the impact on your other accounts.

Password Managers:
1. LastPass:
An easy-to-use password manager that generates and stores complex passwords for each of your accounts.

2. Password:
Provides a secure vault for storing passwords, ensuring you only need to remember one strong master password.

3. KeyPass
Provides an on your computer alternative to using an online password manager providing a little better security to be hacked. It has the ability to store passwords and other data on your hard drive in a data base which is accessible with a master password that only you know. The downside is that you need to back this data base up, which is very easy to do by saving a copy to a USB device or other hard drive, which can be kept separate from your computer.

Periodic Password Changes

While changing passwords regularly was once a common recommendation, recent guidance suggests focusing on creating strong, memorable passwords instead of frequently changing them. However, if a breach occurs, changing passwords promptly is still advisable.

Two-Factor Authentication (2FA)

Adding an extra layer of security, two-factor authentication requires a second form of verification, such as a code sent to your mobile device. Enable 2FA whenever possible to enhance your account security.

Conclusion

Creating strong passwords is a fundamental step in securing your digital life. By incorporating the principles outlined in this chapter, you're building a robust defence against unauthorized access and enhancing your overall cybersecurity resilience. As we progress through "Cybersecurity Simplified," remember that small actions, like crafting a strong password, contribute significantly to your online safety.

Chapter 3: Recognizing Phishing Attacks

In the vast ocean of the internet, phishing is a deceptive technique employed by cybercriminals to lure individuals into revealing sensitive information. This chapter is your guide to understanding phishing attacks, recognizing their tactics, and fortifying your defences against these digital fishing expeditions.
.

What is Phishing?
Phishing is a cybercrime tactic where attackers disguise themselves as trustworthy entities to trick individuals into providing personal information, such as usernames, passwords, and financial details. These deceptive attempts usually come in the form of emails, messages, or websites designed to appear legitimate.

Common Phishing Scenarios:
1. Email Phishing:
Bogus emails imitating reputable organizations, urging recipients to click on links or provide sensitive information.

2. Spear Phishing:
Targeted phishing attacks tailored to specific individuals, often leveraging personal information to appear more convincing.

3. Smishing (SMS Phishing):
Phishing attempts via text messages, tricking individuals into clicking on malicious links or responding with sensitive information.
Recognizing Phishing Attempts

Recognizing Phishing Attempts:
1. Check the Sender's Email Address:
Examine email addresses closely. Legitimate organizations use official domain names; phishing emails may use variations or misspellings.

2. Look for Generic Greetings:
Phishing emails often use generic greetings like "Dear User" instead of personalized greetings with your name.

3. Verify Links Before Clicking:
Hover over links to preview the actual URL. Be cautious if the link appears suspicious or differs from what you expect. Always type the URL into your browser, this is the best way to avoid fake websites. Especially banking.

4. Check for Spelling and Grammar Errors:
Phishing emails often contain spelling and grammar mistakes. Legitimate organizations typically maintain a high standard of communication.

Protecting Yourself from Phishing:
1. Think Before You Click:
Pause and evaluate before clicking on any links, especially in unexpected emails or messages. Verify the sender's authenticity.

2. Verify Requests for Information:
Legitimate organizations rarely request sensitive information via email. Verify such requests independently before responding.

3. Use Email Filtering:
Enable email filtering settings (spam folder) to help detect and filter out potential phishing emails before they reach your inbox.

Reporting Phishing Attempts:

1. Report to Authorities:
If you receive a phishing attempt, report it to the Anti-Phishing Working Group (APWG) or the organization being impersonated.

2. Forward Suspicious Emails:
Forward phishing emails to your email provider. Most providers have mechanisms in place to identify and block such emails. Educating Others

4. Share Awareness:
Educate friends, family, and peers about phishing risks. Sharing awareness helps create a collective defence against these deceptive tactics.

4. Security Training:
Consider participating in cybersecurity awareness programs or workshops to enhance your knowledge and that of those around you.

Conclusion
Phishing attacks thrive on deception, but armed with knowledge, you can become a vigilant defender of your digital fortress. By recognizing the signs of phishing attempts and adopting cautious online behaviour, you're taking a proactive step towards a more secure online experience. As we progress through "Cybersecurity Simplified," remember that staying informed is your greatest defence against digital deception.

Chapter 4: Securing Your Devices

Your devices, whether a computer, smartphone, or tablet, are the gateways to your digital world. Securing them is essential to safeguard your personal information and maintain a resilient defence against cyber threats. In this chapter, we'll explore practical steps to enhance the security of your devices. Importance of Device Security.

Securing your devices is a fundamental aspect of cybersecurity. Your computer and other gadgets store valuable information, making them attractive targets for cybercriminals. Implementing strong security measures ensures that your digital assets remain protected.

Device Security Goals:
1. Preventing Unauthorized Access:
Secure your devices to prevent unauthorized access and protect your personal information.

2. Protecting Data Integrity:
Implement measures to ensure the integrity of your data, preventing unauthorized alterations or deletions.

3. Ensuring Availability:
Maintain the availability of your devices and data by preventing disruptions caused by cyber threats.

Basic Security Measures
1. Operating System Updates:
Regularly update your device's operating system to ensure it has the latest security patches. Enable automatic updates whenever possible.

2. Antivirus Software:
Install reputable antivirus software to detect and remove malicious software that could compromise your device.

3. Firewall Protection:
Activate the built-in firewall on your devices to monitor and control incoming and outgoing network traffic.

Securing Your Computer:
1. User Accounts:
Create strong passwords for user accounts on your computer. Use separate accounts for different users, and avoid using the default "administrator" account for everyday activities. Never leave your computer logged in and always lock your desktop when away from your desk.

2. Encrypting Data:
Enable device encryption to protect your data in case your device is lost or stolen. This ensures that even if unauthorized access occurs, your data remains unreadable.

Smartphone and Tablet Security:
1. Screen Lock:
Set up a secure screen lock (PIN, password, or biometric) on your smartphone and tablet to prevent unauthorized access.

2. App Permissions:
Review and manage app permissions. Only grant necessary permissions to apps, and be cautious about granting access to sensitive information.

3. Remote Wipe:
Enable the remote wipe feature on your smartphone and tablet. This allows you to erase the device's data if it is lost or stolen.

Best Practices for Device Security:
1. Be Wary of Public Wi-Fi:
Avoid accessing sensitive information when connected to public Wi-Fi. If necessary, use a virtual private network (VPN) to encrypt your internet connection. Public Wi-Fi is not safe.

2. Physical Security:
Keep your devices physically secure. Be mindful of where you leave your laptop, smartphone, or tablet, especially in public places.

Periodic Security Audits:
1. Review Settings Regularly:
Periodically review and update your device security settings. Ensure that security features are enabled and configured appropriately.

2. Check for Suspicious Activity:
Monitor your devices for any unusual or suspicious activity. Unrecognized logins or unexpected system behaviour may indicate a security issue.

Conclusion
Securing your devices is a proactive step toward a safer digital experience. By implementing the recommended security measures and staying vigilant, you strengthen your defence against potential cyber threats. As we continue our journey through "Cybersecurity Simplified," remember that device security is an ongoing commitment to protecting your digital assets.

Chapter 5: Social Media Safety

Social media has become an integral part of our lives, connecting us with friends, family, and a vast online community. However, the openness of these platforms also brings potential risks to our personal information. In this chapter, we'll explore strategies to ensure your social media presence remains secure and enjoyable.

The Significance of Social Media Security:
While social media platforms offer avenues for communication and expression, they can also expose personal information to cyber threats. Understanding the risks and adopting security measures allows you to harness the benefits of social media without compromising your privacy.

Key Social Media Risks:
1. Unauthorized Access:
Weak passwords or lax security settings can lead to unauthorized access to your social media accounts.

2. Phishing and Scams:
Cybercriminals may use social media to launch phishing attacks or scams, aiming to trick users into revealing sensitive information.

3. Public Exposure of Personal Information:
Inadvertent sharing of personal details can lead to identity theft or compromise your digital privacy.

Strengthening Your Social Media Security:
1. Review Privacy Settings:
Regularly check and adjust your privacy settings on social media platforms. Limit the visibility of your personal information to only trusted friends.

2. Use Strong, Unique Passwords:
Create strong and unique passwords for each social media account. Avoid using easily guessable information like birthdays or common words.

Secure Your Facebook Account:
1. Privacy Check-up:
Facebook provides a Privacy Check-up feature. Use it to review and adjust who can see your posts, who can contact you, and more.

2. Two-Factor Authentication (2FA):
Enable 2FA on your Facebook account for an additional layer of security. This ensures that even if your password is compromised, an extra step is required for login.

Twitter Security Measures:
1. Secure Your Tweets:
Adjust your Twitter account settings to make your tweets private, visible only to approved followers.

2. Review Connected Apps:
Regularly review and revoke access to third-party apps that are connected to your Twitter account. This minimizes potential security risks.

Instagram Account Security:
1. Private Account Setting:
Switch your Instagram account to private mode, allowing only approved followers to view your posts.

2. Manage Third-Party Apps:
Similar to Twitter, periodically review and remove third-party apps with access to your Instagram account.

General Social Media Safety Tips:
1. Be Mindful of Sharing:
Avoid oversharing personal information, such as your address or phone number, on social media platforms.

2. Recognize Scams and Phishing Attempts:
Stay vigilant for phishing attempts and scams. Be cautious about clicking on links from unknown sources.

3. Regularly Monitor Account Activity:
Periodically review your social media account activity to identify any unauthorized access or suspicious behaviour.

Conclusion
By implementing these social media safety measures, you can enjoy the benefits of connectivity without compromising your security. As we continue to progress through "Cybersecurity Simplified," remember that being mindful of your digital footprint contributes significantly to your overall online safety.

Chapter 6: Data Backups and Recovery

Imagine losing all your digital photos, important documents, and cherished memories in an instant. It's a nightmare scenario, but with proper data backup and recovery strategies, you can safeguard against such disasters. In this chapter, we'll explore the importance of data backups and guide you through the process of securing your valuable digital assets.

Data loss can occur due to various reasons, including hardware failures, software issues, cyberattacks, or accidental deletions. Data backups serve as a safety net, ensuring that even if the unexpected happens, your information remains intact and recoverable.

Common Causes of Data Loss:
1. Hardware Failures:
Hard drive failures, unexpected power outages, or hardware malfunctions can lead to data loss.

2. Software Issues:
Bugs, glitches, or corrupted software may compromise your data.

3. Cyberattacks:
Ransomware attacks or other forms of malware can encrypt or destroy your data.

Creating Effective Data Backups:
1. Establish a Regular Backup Schedule:
Set up a routine for backing up your data, whether it's daily, weekly, or monthly. Consistency is key.

2. Choose the Right Backup Storage:
Select a reliable and secure backup storage solution. This could be an external hard drive, cloud storage service, or a combination of both.

Types of Data Backups:
1. Full Backups:
A complete copy of all selected data, providing a comprehensive snapshot of your files and folders.

2. Incremental Backups:
Backs up only the data that has changed since the last backup. Efficient for saving storage space and quicker backup times.

3. Google Drive:
Offers seamless integration with Google Workspace apps and provides a reliable cloud storage solution.

4. Dropbox:
Allows you to synchronize and backup files, providing easy access from multiple devices.

Recovery Strategies:
1. Regularly Test Backups:
Periodically test the restoration process to ensure your backups are functional and can be successfully recovered.

2. Data Recovery Software:
Explore data recovery software options that can help retrieve lost files in case of accidental deletion or corruption.

Securing Your Backups:
1. Encrypt Backup Data:
Implement encryption on your backups to add an extra layer of security, especially for sensitive information.

2. Password Protection:
Password-protect your backups to restrict unauthorized access.

Creating a Recovery Plan:
1. Document Your Backup Strategy:
Maintain documentation of your backup strategy, including schedules, storage locations, and recovery procedures.

2. Emergency Procedures:
Develop a plan for emergency situations, outlining steps to take in the event of data loss or system failures.

Conclusion
Data backups are your digital insurance policy, offering peace of mind in an unpredictable digital landscape. By incorporating these backup and recovery strategies into your cybersecurity practices, you not only protect your digital assets but also ensure a swift recovery in the face of unforeseen challenges. As we continue through "Cybersecurity Simplified," remember that a well-executed backup plan is a cornerstone of your digital resilience.

Chapter 7: Staying Safe on Public Wi-Fi

Public Wi-Fi is a convenient way to stay connected on the go, but it comes with its own set of security risks. In this chapter, we'll explore the potential dangers of using public Wi-Fi and provide you with practical tips to ensure your online activities remain secure, even when connected to unsecured networks.

The Risks of Public Wi-Fi:
1. Man-in-the-Middle Attacks:
Cybercriminals can intercept data transmitted between your device and the Wi-Fi network, leading to unauthorized access to your information.

2. Rogue Hotspots:
Attackers may set up rogue Wi-Fi hotspots with names similar to legitimate networks, tricking users into connecting to malicious networks.

3. Unencrypted Connections:
Public Wi-Fi networks often lack encryption, making it easier for hackers to intercept sensitive data.

Practical Tips for Secure Public Wi-Fi Use:
1. Use Virtual Private Networks (VPNs):
VPNs encrypt your internet connection, adding an extra layer of security. Consider using a reputable VPN service, especially when accessing sensitive information.

2. Avoid Accessing Sensitive Data:
Refrain from accessing sensitive information such as online banking or confidential emails while connected to public Wi-Fi.

Configuring Your Device for Public Wi-Fi:
1. Turn Off Sharing:
Disable file and printer sharing as well as public folder sharing to minimize the risk of unauthorized access to your device.

2. Enable Firewall Protection:
Activate your device's built-in firewall to monitor and control incoming and outgoing network traffic.

Web Browsing Best Practices:
1. Use HTTPS Connections:
Whenever possible, access websites that use "https://" in the URL. This indicates a secure, encrypted connection.

2. Beware of Unsecured Networks:
Be cautious when connecting to open, unsecured networks. Confirm the network's legitimacy with staff if you're in a public place. As a rule, I don't use Public Wi-Fi for this reason.

Mobile Device Security:
1. Turn Off Auto-Connect:
Disable the auto-connect feature on your mobile device to prevent automatic connections to open Wi-Fi networks.

2. Forget Network After Use:
Once you've finished using a public Wi-Fi network, manually disconnect and "forget" the network to avoid automatic reconnection.

Educating Others:
1. Share Awareness:
Educate friends, family, and colleagues about the risks associated with public Wi-Fi and the importance of adopting security measures.

2. Encourage VPN Usage:
Advocate for the use of VPNs among those in your network, emphasizing their role in enhancing online security.

Conclusion
While public Wi-Fi offers convenience, it's crucial to approach it with caution and implement security measures to protect your data. By following the practical tips outlined in this chapter, you can navigate public Wi-Fi networks safely and minimize the risks associated with connecting to unsecured environments. As we continue through "Cybersecurity Simplified," remember that staying vigilant in various online scenarios contributes to your overall digital safety.

Chapter 8: Recognizing Online Scams

The online world is rife with scams designed to exploit unsuspecting individuals. In this chapter, we'll delve into the realm of online scams, providing you with insights on common tactics used by cybercriminals and empowering you to recognize and avoid falling victim to their deceptive schemes.

Understanding Online Scams

Online scams take various forms, each with the common goal of tricking individuals into providing sensitive information, such as passwords, financial details, or personal data. Recognizing these scams is essential for safeguarding your digital well-being.

Common Types of Online Scams:

1. Phishing Scams:

Deceptive attempts to trick individuals into revealing sensitive information by posing as trustworthy entities, often through emails or fake websites.

2. Online Shopping Scams:

Fraudulent websites or sellers offering fake products or services to deceive consumers.

3. Tech Support Scams:

Calls or pop-up messages claiming to be from tech support, urging individuals to pay for unnecessary services or providing remote access to their devices.

Recognizing Red Flags:
1. Urgency and Pressure:
Scams often create a sense of urgency, pressuring individuals to act quickly without proper consideration.

2. Too Good to Be True Offers:
Be sceptical of offers that seem too good to be true. Scammers use enticing offers to lure victims. If it seems too good to be true, then ignore the email/offer.

Protecting Yourself from Online Scams:
1. Verify Email Addresses:
Check the legitimacy of email addresses, especially when receiving unexpected emails. Legitimate organizations use official domain names.

2. Independently Verify Requests:
Independently verify requests for sensitive information, especially if received via email or unexpected messages.

3. Use Reputable Online Sellers:
When shopping online, stick to reputable websites and sellers. Check reviews and ratings before making purchases. A good way to protect your credit card is to use something like PayPal, that you never have to type your card number and they like to protect their users.

Reporting Scams:
1. Federal Trade Commission (FTC):
Report online scams to the FTC, providing details about the scam and your interactions.

2. Internet Crime Complaint Center (IC3) :
File a complaint with the IC3 for internet-related scams.
Educating Others

3. Share Information:
Spread awareness about common online scams among friends, family, and colleagues to collectively build a resilient defence.

4. Promote Cybersecurity Education:
Advocate for cybersecurity education in schools, workplaces, and communities to empower individuals with the knowledge to recognize and avoid scams.

Conclusion
By being vigilant and informed, you can navigate the digital landscape with confidence and avoid falling prey to online scams. Understanding the tactics employed by cybercriminals and adopting a cautious approach to online interactions contribute to a safer digital experience. As we progress through "Cybersecurity Simplified," remember that knowledge is your most powerful tool in the fight against online deception.

Chapter 9: Safeguarding Your Personal Identity

Your personal identity is an asset, and protecting it in the digital age is paramount. In this chapter, we'll explore the significance of your personal identity, the risks associated with identity theft, and practical steps to safeguard yourself against potential threats.

The Importance of Personal Identity Protection:
Your personal identity encompasses a wide range of information, from your name and address to financial details and online accounts. Safeguarding this identity is crucial for preventing identity theft, fraud, and other cybercrimes.

Components of Personal Identity:
1. Personal Information:
Name, address, phone number, and date of birth.

2. Financial Details:
Bank account numbers, credit card information, and social security numbers.

3. Online Accounts:
Usernames, passwords, and other credentials used to access online services.

Risks of Identity Theft:
1. Financial Loss:
Identity theft can lead to unauthorized financial transactions, draining your accounts or opening credit in your name.

2. Legal Consequences:

Criminals may commit crimes using your identity, leading to legal consequences for which you may be held responsible.

3. Emotional Toll:

The emotional toll of identity theft can be significant, causing stress, anxiety, and a sense of violation.

Practical Steps for Identity Protection:
1. Secure Personal Documents:

Store important documents, such as passports and social security cards, in a secure and locked location.

2. Use Strong Passwords:

Employ strong, unique passwords for all your online accounts to prevent unauthorized access.

3. Monitor Financial Statements:

Regularly review bank statements, credit card statements, and credit reports for any unauthorized transactions or suspicious activity.

Online Identity Protection:
1. Enable Two-Factor Authentication (2FA):

Activate 2FA on your online accounts to add an extra layer of security, requiring a second form of verification.

2. Be Cautious with Personal Information Sharing:

Limit the amount of personal information shared online, especially on social media platforms.

Recognizing Identity Theft Warning Signs:
1. Unexplained Financial Transactions:
Unexpected withdrawals or charges on your financial accounts.

2. Receiving Bills for Unfamiliar Accounts:
Receiving statements or bills for accounts you did not open.

3. Unexpected Denials of Credit:
Being denied credit or loans without a clear reason.

Reporting Identity Theft:
1. Federal Trade Commission (FTC):
Report identity theft to your relevant Countries Government organisation, providing details about the incident and steps taken.

2. Credit Bureaus:
Contact credit bureaus to place a fraud alert on your credit reports.

Educating Others:
1. Family and Friends:
Share information about identity protection with family and friends to collectively enhance awareness and security.

2. Workplace Awareness Programs:
Advocate for identity theft awareness programs in workplaces to educate employees about potential risks.

Conclusion

Protecting your personal identity is an ongoing commitment to ensuring a secure and resilient digital life. By implementing the recommended steps and staying vigilant, you empower yourself to navigate the online world with confidence. As we get closer to the end of "Cybersecurity Simplified," remember that your personal identity is worth safeguarding, and your efforts contribute to a safer digital community.

As we conclude our exploration of Cybersecurity Simplified," it is essential to address the crucial aspect of building a secure and positive online presence. Your actions and interactions in the digital realm leave a lasting footprint, and understanding how to navigate this space responsibly is key to fostering a secure and enjoyable online experience.

Mindful Digital Citizenship:
1. Choose Strong Usernames:
When creating accounts on various platforms, opt for usernames that do not reveal personal information. Avoid using easily guessable names or details that could compromise your privacy.

2. Craft Robust Passwords:
Maintain the habit of creating strong, unique passwords for each online account. This not only protects your accounts but also contributes to your overall digital security.

Engaging in Positive Online Communities:
1. Be Respectful and Inclusive:
Foster a positive online environment by being respectful and inclusive in your interactions. Avoid engaging in cyberbullying or spreading negativity.

2. Verify Information Before Sharing:
Help combat the spread of misinformation by verifying the accuracy of information before sharing it. Be a responsible contributor to online conversations.

Safeguarding Your Digital Reputation:
1. Review Privacy Settings:
Regularly review and update the privacy settings on your social media accounts. Adjust the visibility of your posts and personal information to control who can access your profile.

2. Think Before You Post:
Consider the potential impact of your posts on your digital reputation. Once something is shared online, it can be challenging to completely erase its presence.

Protecting Personal Information:
1. Limit Personal Details:
Avoid oversharing personal information such as your address, phone number, or financial details. Share only what is necessary and be mindful of the potential consequences.

2. Secure Your Online Accounts:
Enable two-factor authentication (2FA) whenever possible. This adds an extra layer of security to your accounts, reducing the risks of unauthorised access.

Responsible Online Branding:
1. Craft a Positive Digital Image:
Whether for personal or professional reasons, project a positive digital image. This contributes to a strong online presence and can be beneficial for various aspects of your life.

2. Google Yourself:
Regularly search for your name online to monitor your digital footprint. Address any inaccuracies or unwanted content that may affect your online reputation.

Conclusion

Your online presence is an extension of yourself in the digital world. By implementing the practices discussed in this chapter, you're not only enhancing your cybersecurity but also contributing to a positive and respectful online community.

Remember that responsible digital citizenship is a shared responsibility, and each individual's actions shape the collective experience of the digital realm.

As you embark on your journey in the online space, carry with you the knowledge and principles learned throughout this guide.

A secure and positive online presence is not only a reflection of your commitment to cybersecurity but also a testament to your role as a responsible digital citizen.

Happy Navigating!

www.ingramcontent.com/pod-product-compliance
Lightning Source LLC
Chambersburg PA
CBHW072226290526
45794CB00007B/2902